Disclaimer

The information contained with
informational and entertainment purposes only. I am not an
attorney. The information provided in this manual is only my
opinion. These opinions are based on a combination of my own
personal experiences, experiences in communicating with others
in the industry, and researching online resources to make my
own decisions.

You should view everything I am about to say as entertainment
only. I cannot be held responsible for any of your individual
results, good, bad or indifferent.

You have to do your own research and due diligence as well as
make your own informed decisions on how to move forward with
the information provided.

Contents

Introduction

The online used car flipper and aspiring car salesman movement is strong!

Individuals who bought new or used cars and eventually sold them privately has always been a thing. There are folks who bought a car brand new, drove it for 15 years, put 200,000 miles on it and eventually sold it for an average private party car resale book value. There are also folks who bought a used car for much less than the average private party car resale book value and sold it three weeks later for a significant profit; while never intending to keep the car as a daily driver. There are also folks that fall somewhere in between the two scenarios aforementioned.

And of course, there are car dealers. There are dealers who own an authorized car dealership with a 30,000 square foot lot holding 450 new and used cars in inventory. There are also dealers who own a struggling "buy here, pay here" used car lot holding 15 cars in inventory, 13 of which will stop working within two weeks of driving it off of their car lot. There are also dealers that fall somewhere in between the two scenarios aforementioned.

Regardless of what category the individual falls within the scenarios listed above, every one of them has one thing in common. They are looking to make money from the sale of their car. They have to advertise it. Someone has to come look at it. They must negotiate a deal for the value of the car. Then they must close the sale and complete the title work.

The greatest thing about the used car market is that no individual car, nor its "value," is ever equal to itself or to another vehicle. While there are websites, car guides, forums, etc, that can provide a general "value" of a vehicle, the car is only ever worth what someone is willing to pay for it.

The worst thing about the used car market is that the industry has become saturated with individuals who have not had the training and/or have not had the experiences, failures, and successes that come along with buying and selling cars to maximize their profit potential. Imagine being in a NFL football stadium where every seat is occupied. Now imagine every single spectator in the stands is screaming at the top of their lungs, "buy my car!" Imagine that there is one individual standing in the center of the field on the 50 yard line. Imagine that this is a potential car buyer in the private party sector who wants to buy a used car. This car buyer is looking around the stadium. All they hear is noise. From time to time, they see a banner. Perhaps they see someone in the crowd doing something unusual that catches their attention. Perhaps they see a very attractive person of the opposite sex. Now imagine that everyone in the stand is a used car salesman. This is what the used car market has become. A saturated industry where everyone wants to make some money selling their car to that person standing on the 50 yard line.

This manual was written for you, the excited entrepreneur, who wants to learn how to get the guy on the 50 yard line to notice you amongst the crowd, get him to like you over everyone else, negotiate a deal to maximize your profit, then sell your car to him as effortlessly as possible.

Goal of the Manual

The fundamental goal of this manual is to provide you the tools to accomplish the following:
1) Maximize your profit while mitigating your risk as a private party car salesman

The secondary goals of this manual is to provide you the tools to accomplish the following:
1) Learn what it takes to get started as a private party car salesman
2) Learn how much you can reasonably expect to earn annually as a private party car salesman
3) Learn how to identify a good car deal as the buyer
4) Learn how to research the buyer or seller on the other end of the transaction; while acquiring public data about them prior to meeting them
5) Learn how to negotiate a deal as both a private party buyer and a private party seller
6) Learn how to complete a proper car inspection prior to your purchase
7) Learn how to advertise your car more efficiently than your competitors
8) Learn where to identify the forms associated with your title transfer and how to fill them out properly
9) Learn the difference between buying and selling cars in the private party market as opposed to becoming a licensed car dealer or wholesaler
10) Evaluate your own personal strengths and opportunities to maximize your confidence level

The final goal of this manual is for you to understand why my strategies are unique and superior to my competitors. As you will learn, anyone can do this. However, many getting started will follow guidance from my competitors that will cause them to be unethical, cause them to lie to their potential buyers and/or cause them to break both federal and state laws. The guidance I will provide you will accomplish maximizing your profit on each deal; while mitigating the risk of investing in bad cars and doing business with shady and dangerous people.

Table of Contents

Chapter One

Getting started – how do I become a private party car salesman?

Starting a business is difficult. If it were easy, then we'd have way more business owners and not as many nine-to-five hourly wage earners as we do now. Historical data has proven that over 90% of businesses fail within the first two years of getting started. Why is that? There could be a number of reasons. First, perhaps they failed to develop and adhere to a good business plan. Maybe they failed to plan out their strategy for the first year, two or five. Second, perhaps they invested way too much money up front and eventually were unable to pay back the excessive amount of money they initially invested. Third, maybe they continuously failed to earn a potential buyer's business. Maybe it was a combination of all these things.

One of the greatest things about selling used cars privately is that it does not require a lot of money to get started. Nor does it require a college degree, high school diploma or big building to keep your cars. You can buy and sell cars privately in your driveway. You can be a stay at home Mom who watches the kids by day and sells cars for profit on nights and weekends. You can be a high school graduate who decided to take a few years off before going to college; doing this on the side to make some extra money. You can be a senior executive vice president at a major corporation who likes to buy big motor sports cars in the winter, drive them in the summer, and sell them after having fun with them. The types of people who can buy and sell cars are endless. Anyone can do it, as long as you have a driver's license. You do not need a dealer's license. You do not need a specific degree. You do not need a specific certification. What you will need is either a car that you own outright with the car title in hand (you are the seller) or a small amount of money (you are the buyer) to get started.

So how does one even become a private party car salesman to begin with?

You will start your journey in private party car sales as either a buyer or a seller. Review each of the scenarios below. You will fall under one of them. Once you determine which one you are currently, then you will take the action steps in the later chapters of the manual to move forward.

Scenario # 1: The private party salesman who does not currently own a car to sell:

In order to sell a car privately, you obviously need a car to sell privately. Let's assume that you are not currently a car owner. What would you do? The first step is to generate $5,000.00. Here are a few suggestions on how to earn the capital to start your private party car selling business:

1) Take out an unsecured loan (automatically closed once it is paid off) or a re-accessible line of credit (meaning you can use the credit limit more than once

after it is paid off) with a credit union or local bank. You may have to call the bank, submit an application online or walk into a local branch to apply for your funds. Contingent upon your credit history and ability to repay the loan, the bank should typically be able to approve you within a few days of submitting your application at most. The bank can typically give you cash in hand for the full amount once the loan or line of credit is approved.

2) Borrow money from a family member or friend. Offer to pay them back in weekly or monthly payments over a specified period of time.

3) Earn an hourly income at a job and save the money yourself.

Whichever way you decide to generate your initial $5,000 would be fine. This will be the starting point for your private party car selling business. The good news is that you will not need much more than this if you follow the guidance I will offer you throughout the manual.

I want to make a quick note. I am providing you a blueprint to remain as ethical and debt-free as possible throughout your private party car buying and selling career; while also mitigating the risk associated with bad car buying investments. There are many competitors in the industry that will persuade you to start with a smaller investment, $2,000 for example. If you are inexperienced in the field of auto mechanics, and do not have the expertise to complete car repairs correctly and efficiently, then I would highly recommend that you start with a $5,000 initial investment. It is very difficult to purchase a reliable car for $2,000 or less in the private party sector.

You are now a buyer in the world of private party car buying and selling.

Scenario # 2: The private party salesman who owns a car they want to sell, but does not have it paid off yet:

If you currently have a car that is owned by the bank, then you do not "own" the car, per se. You will want to pay the secured auto loan off in its entirety before you can sell it. This can be accomplished by following the same steps in Scenario # 1. Once you have paid off the lien, then the bank will send you the car title in the mail. You will typically receive the title anywhere within one to six weeks of paying off the car loan. This will vary depending on your bank.

Once you receive your car title, you are now a seller in the world of car buying and selling.

Scenario # 3: The private party salesman who owns their car outright and has the car title in hand

You, my friend, have a very nice situation to get started. You are automatically starting off as a seller in the world of car buying and selling.

Chapter Two

How much money can I really make buying and selling cars in the private party market?

The fundamental and honest answer is about $7,000 to $10,000 a year if you buy and title cars as a private party in your name only. Each state has different laws regarding how many cars can be bought and sold by one individual person. I would highly recommend researching the state in which you reside to determine how many cars you can buy and sell within a year. You must also consider that certain states may not be as concerned with the amount of cars you sell, as they are more concerned with the actual profit you are showing on each car. In some states, they even go so far as to review their complaints database to see if neighbors are complaining about their "car dealer" neighbors having 20 cars sitting around their four car driveway. Just like everything else in life, there are exceptions to every rule.

Exception Rule # 1
If someone is married, then they may have considered titling cars in their spouse's name. This would provide them the ability to title eight cars per year as opposed to four cars per year, assuming that each car was titled only in one person's name.

Exception Rule # 2
If someone has a family member or friend who was willing to have a car or cars titled in their name, then they may have considered titling four additional cars for each

person they have a relationship with. Some of these folks have even gone so far as to give the friend or family member an extra $200 to $500 per car to make it worth their time.

Exception Rule # 3
Someone may purchase a car from a private party seller; asking them to only date the title and not sign it. Then, they would never actually get the car titled in their name or pay the required state taxes on the vehicle. Then, they would immediately sell it to a third party, have the third party sign the title and get it tagged in their name. This is considered "floating the title." The original buyer was a "ghost" in the transaction, since they signed the vehicle to their name.

NOTE: I would highly recommend not getting involved in these exception scenarios, especially the third one. The first two exceptions can be deemed both "illegal" and/or "unethical" depending on who you ask. The third exception is illegal no matter what way you look at it.

The average profit on a car flip is about $2,000 net for the average private party car salesman considering the following things:
1) Their experience or lack thereof in car repairs and auto body work
2) Their cost to tax, tag, title, inspect and insure a car
3) Their expenses to advertise their car, when applicable
4) Their costs for car repairs

The reason I recommended an initial $5,000 investment is because anyone can find a deal where they would start out paying $4,500 cash for a decent car to flip. While nothing is guaranteed, a $4,500 car that is purchased from a reputable and honest seller can yield having no issues in the three weeks to a month it takes you to sell it.

Scenario # 1
2012 Chevrolet Sonic LTZ with only 33,500 miles

The Chevy Sonic is a pretty basic hatchback. It has power windows, four doors and can be found with an automatic transmission. Even being a nine year old car, it has very low miles, is reliable and has no known mechanical or cosmetic issues. Let's say you purchased this car in cash from a retired military woman who has three cars and simply wants to move it out of her driveway quickly. After doing your homework and investigating the seller, you determine the car is worth $7,800 in the private party sector. Let's also assume she is asking $5,200 for the car. You meet her, test drive the car, determine it's in very good condition with no issues and offer her $4,300 in cash. She counteroffers and says she can sell it for $4,800. Then you counteroffer again with an offer of $4,500 which she accepts.

Next, you've taxed, tagged and titled the car in your name. It cost you $360 total. You had the car inspected and that ran you $50. You also opted to pay car insurance on it. Your total expenses to own the car was $4,960. You received the title in the mail 10 days after purchasing the car from the initial seller. You advertised the car, had a father of a 16 year old girl come to look at it, and then he bought from you for $7,200. Here would be your total profit margin on this car:

Cost of Car	$4,500
Taxes, Tags, Title	$360
Inspection	$50
Car Insurance (Pro-rated)	$50
Total Expenses	$4,960
Sales Price	$7,200
Net Profit (Sales Price minus Total Expenses)	**$2,240**

The decision will ultimately be up to you to determine whether or not you want to buy and sell cars privately or buy and sell cars as a dealer. Both the similarities and differences between private sellers and car dealers or wholesalers will be explained in chapter 7 of the manual.

Chapter 3

I am the buyer – how do I find a good deal?

Do you recall the fundamental goal of the manual? If so, what was it?

If you don't remember, then I will remind you. The fundamental goal of this manual is to maximize your profit while mitigating risk as a private party car salesman. All your profit is made on the buy, not on the sell. I will repeat. All your profit is made on the buy, not on the sell. I will repeat. All your profit is made on the buy, not on the sell.

This is the most crucial step in being successful as a private party car salesman. I will teach you how to find a good deal by incorporating each the following action steps into your car buying process:

1) **3.1 – Kelley Blue Book (KBB):** Learn how to use Kelley Blue Book to determine values: Dealer trade-in, Dealer instant cash offer, private party values and dealer retail values.
2) **3.2 – Finding Deals on the Internet:** Learn how to use the top five internet websites to locate deals: Craigslist, Cars.com, Autotrader.com, Facebook Marketplace and eBay Motors.
3) **3.3 – Carfax reports:** Learn how to use them and understand why they are important

4) **3.4 - Know the Seller before you meet the Seller**: Learn how to use external websites like white pages, Zillow.com, LinkedIn and Facebook to investigate the buyer or seller before you meet them.

5) **3.5 - The Art of the Deal: Negotiation as the Buyer**: Always research and determine your ceiling amount. Never exceed this amount within your negotiation. Understand that you are never wrong to walk away from a deal, no matter how wonderful, sexy and profitable you think it might be. There will be others. Go with your gut. If your gut tells you to walk away, then do it. If your gut tells you to offer cash and close the deal, then proceed with caution to the steps to get you to finalize the deal.

6) **3.6 - The Art of the Deal: Negotiation as the Seller**: There is always a buyer. You just have to find them. If you can get a potential buyer to pull up in your driveway, then you've most likely sold your car.

3.1 - Kelley Blue Book (KBB)

The Kelley Blue Book value of cars is more or less the cornerstone of car values. While there are other websites available that offer car values such as NADA, Carfax and Edmunds.com, KBB is the resource that most people use. Therefore, it is a great practice to understand how to navigate their website while understanding what you are looking for. We will start with private party values, as this is typically what you will review when buying and selling cars.

KBB Private Party Values

There are four KBB private party values: Fair, Good, Very Good and Excellent. KBB provides a description for each category, however they are pretty general. A vast majority of cars are valued at "Good" simply because of the description. NOTE: KBB is simply a reference guide. It is not an exact science.

IMPORTANT: When determining the maximum value you want to pay for a car in the private party car buying world, you should aim to pay no more than $600 below fair value on KBB private party value. The sweet spot to make a great profit is to buy the car within $800 to $1,100 under the fair private party value on KBB.

There will be exceptions to this rule depending on things such as 1) limited supply and enormous demand of the vehicle you want to purchase, 2) how quick you want to flip it, and 3) whether or not you want to drive it for a while before you sell it.

How to use KBB:
1) Go to kbb.com
2) Click on My Car's Value
3) Click on Get Trade-In Value
4) You will be prompted to select general information about your car: year, make, model and mileage. Fill this information out, then click Next

Here is an example for a 2010 Honda Accord LX-P with 100,000 miles:

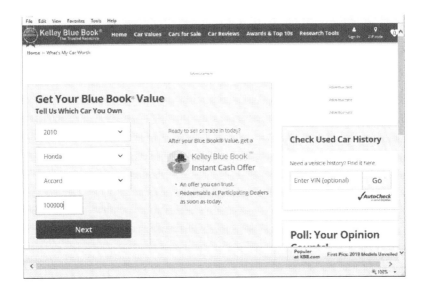

5) Now, put in the zip code. We will use Raleigh, North Carolina 27513 as an example.

6) Select the category for your vehicle. We will use a sedan (four door).

7) Once you select the category, you will select a radio button for the exact style of your vehicle. You will want to try your best to select the correct style because this could have an impact on the values. We will select the LX-P style. It is the lowest priced.

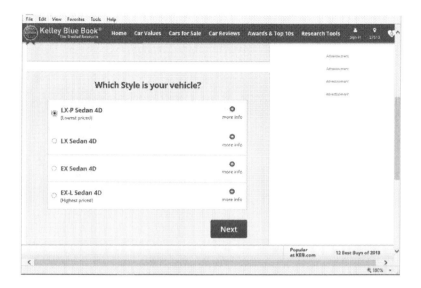

8) The next screen will ask you if you want to either select your options or price with standard equipment. It is a good practice to choose the Select your Options radio button. Certain options will have an impact on the value of the vehicle you are researching. For our example, several radio buttons within the Select your Options field are pre-selected for you. Typically these are options that come standard with the vehicle. There are three categories that you will review:

a. Mechanical (includes engine size, drivetrain, braking and steering)

b. Interior (includes radio/entertainment, comfort and convenience and seats)

c. Exterior (includes safety/security, lighting, wheels/tires and body packages)

d. Color (this may have an impact on price since certain colors are more favorable than others

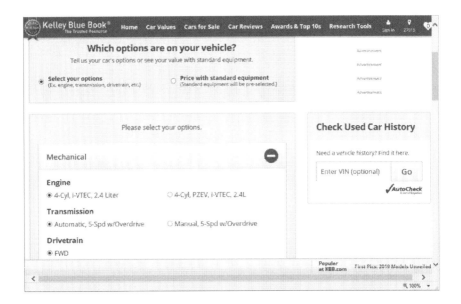

9) Once you've selected your color, you will be prompted to select the condition of the vehicle. Start with the Fair value. Click on it, then select Next.

10) KBB will automatically calculate the value of your car. You will notice that there are four tabs above the Trade-in Range. They are:
   a. Instant Cash Offer
   b. Trade-In Value
   c. Private Party Value
   d. Donate Your Car

11) Click on the Private Party Value tab. You will notice that the "Private Party Range" for this particular vehicle in Fair condition is $5,847 to $7,540 (green). The average of these two figures is the actual Private Party Value of $6,694 (white). Since we are going to work smarter and not harder when we look for deals, we can just be concerned with the Private Party Value disclosed in white, which is

$6,694. This is the Fair value number that we want to write down. We will need this to consider what we'd be willing to pay for a used car in the private party market. NOTE: Keep in mind that depending on when you are reading the manual, the value of this vehicle may have changed significantly if you are trying to recalculate what I did.

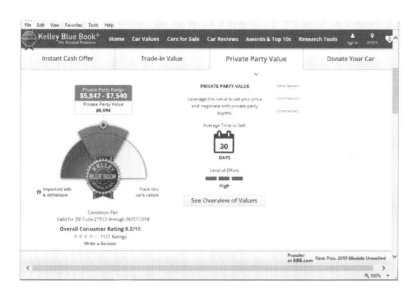

12) Now, go back to the KBB home page. You need to calculate the values for Good, Very Good, and Excellent. Not to worry. I've already done it for us in this example.

KBB values for 2010 Honda Accord LX-P (100,000 Miles)	
Fair	$6,694
Good	$7,196
Very Good	$7,707
Excellent	$8,360
Average	**$7,489**

Trade-In Value	$5,510
NOTE: The Very Good trade-in value on KBB (not private party) for this car is significantly less (about $1,200 under private party fair value). This is the amount of money that the current seller could expect to receive if they either traded their car in or sold it directly at a car dealership.	

13) IMPORTANT: Remember that our goal is to make all our money on the buy. Think back to our target amount of what we want to buy the car for. Do you remember the amount? Do you remember what KBB category to consider when calculating that amount? Our sweet spot to buy a car from a private party seller is $800 to $1,100 under the fair private party value. So how do we do that if the average of KBB on private party is $7,489 and $1,000 under fair value is $5,694? That is a difference of $1,795? Stay tuned and keep reading...

3.2 – Finding Deals on the Internet

Now that we've received a crash course in determining the value of cars we may want to buy, the next step is to figure out where to find deals. There are many different websites that we can look at. However, remember that we want to work smarter, not harder. There are four websites which are the bread and butter of good deals. I've listed them in the order of importance. While they all add their own particular value, some may or may not be as lucrative as the others. We will explain each one in detail.

We will explain the strengths and opportunities of each website:

1) Craigslist
2) Autotrader
3) Cars.com
4) Facebook Marketplace

Craigslist

Craigslist is the king of all private party car buying websites. When starting out in the private party car buying industry, this is the best place to start your search to buy your first car. Craigslist is a free advertising site. Both dealers and private party sellers can open a Craigslist account through an email and password, upload over 20 pictures of their car, write a description of what they are selling and provide their contact information so a potential buyer can contact them.

There are several advantages of using Craigslist to the private party car buyer. Craigslist makes it very easy to target what you are looking for through the search field and filters available. Also, each Craigslist location covers a good part of the demographic (cities) on where you are searching. The filters include:

1) Filter by private owner, dealer or both
2) Filter by miles from zip code
3) Filter by price
4) Filter by model year
5) Filter by odometer reading
6) Filter by engine size (cylinders)

7) Filter by drivetrain (FWD, AWD, RWD, 4X4)
8) Filter by paint color
9) Filter by title status (clean, salvage, rebuilt, lien, parts)
10) Filter by transmission (manual/stick shift, automatic, automanual)
11) Filter by type (convertible, sedan, coupe, pickup, etc)

Using key word searches, you can search precisely for what you are looking for. While the search word and subsequent filter possibilities are endless, I would recommend using a few fundamental keywords and filters to find the best deals. I will also explain why you should use them.

Let's go all the way back to Chapter 1 Scenario # 1 where we are a buyer with $5,000 cash in hand. We will use this as our scenario for all the internet channel examples to follow.

1) Original owner: Regardless of the make, model, year, miles, etc, these are the two most important search words that you can use when purchasing a car from a private seller. Original owner cars means that no one else owned the car besides them. That means that proper maintenance and upkeep has most likely been completed. It also means that the car most likely has maintenance records to evidence how it has been cared for. It also means that it hasn't been flipped by a private party car salesman.

2) Price: Using the price filter, I would highly recommend starting with a $3,500 minimum and a $7,000 maximum if we are looking to spend no more than $4,500 for a used car. Never start with a price of $0 or $1. In fact, never start with a price under $1,500. As you will learn with time, experience and knowledge within this business, many of the crooks out there will put their "price" as $15. What they really mean is $15,000. That is not within our price point, so we're not going to waste our time even having them pop up in our search. We are putting $7,000 as our maximum, because there is always a possibility that we can buy a car advertised at $7,000 for $4,500. It is rare, but it could happen depending on the car. Furthermore, you'll want to correlate the difference in what you can get between a car listed at $5,000 versus a similar car listed at $7,000. This is how you will better learn the business.

3) Model Year: Using the model year filter, we want to target current generation cars. As a general rule of thumb, I'd recommend staying within a 10 year window of the current year. Cars that are older than 10 years historically have more issues than those that are younger. Again, we make all our money on the buy. We want to buy smart while mitigating unnecessary risk. If we buy a 15 year old car with major rust or ball joint wear, then much of the potential profit gets used in car repairs.

4) Odometer: Using the odometer filter, I'd recommend starting with a minimum value of 2,500 miles. First, you are not going to find a good car

with less than 2,500 miles for $5,000. Many of the con artists will put 250 as the mileage in their advertisement. When you open their ad, the car has 250,000 miles. No Bueno. We don't want to buy that car, so let's keep it off our search. We also want to max out at 100,000 miles as our ceiling. While it becomes more difficult to buy a car at the $5,000 price point under 100,000 miles, it absolutely can be done. Once cars start exceeding 100,000 miles, they start needing some of the bigger maintenance requirements. These include ball joints, control arms, timing belts, transmissions, etc. Many original owner private sellers will want to sell their cars prior to having to invest big money into these larger maintenance requirements. We don't want these requirements to become our problem prior to selling it if we buy it. Finally, most buyers who may be looking to buy a car would overlook our car if we were the seller. Most of the general public (not including private party car flippers) want to buy cars under 100,000 miles, so they won't search for cars with more than that.

5) Title status: Using the title status, I would highly recommend searching by "clean" only. Salvage and rebuilt titles typically are a result of water (electrical) damage and/or theft recovery. No Bueno. Stay away from them.

6) Transmission: Using the transmission filter, if you are new to the game then I would recommend searching only by an automatic transmission. This new generation doesn't want a stick shift in their right hand while driving, they want a cell phone in

their right hand while driving. You will have more success flipping a car with an automatic transmission than you would flipping a car with a manual transmission. Of course, there are exceptions to every rule, such as older Jeep Wranglers and Ford Mustangs.

7) The other filters are more or less optional. They don't need to be filled out. In fact, I would highly recommend sticking with the search words and filters above to identify potential cars that you might consider purchasing.

Here is an example of a search using the criteria above in Raleigh, North Carolina:

Disadvantages of Craigslist: Because it is free advertising, beware of the Con Artists!

Here are a few tricks that the con artists will use. Keep an eye out for these, as they will be beneficial to weed out the nonsense so you can work smarter and not harder:

1) If you look at pictures of the car and there is no license plate, then they are a con artist car dealer pretending to be a private party seller. It usually means that the car is neither registered nor inspected. Hence, no license plate or dealer plate on the back.

2) If you search by "original owner," and the description leads you to reading something that says "original miles" with the word owner somewhere else in the advertisement, then they are a con artist.

3) If they say "Just testing the waters," they are a con artist.

4) If they say something like, "this is a clean car," or "interior and exterior are clean," then they are a con artist.

5) If they do not provide a phone number to call or text you, only an email address, then it is because they are a con artist trying to fly under the radar of government/DMV scrutiny.

6) If they say "up for sale," then they are a con artist.

7) If they provide an inaccurate price or odometer reading, then they are a con artist.

8) If they advertise pictures in a car lot with other cars for sale, then they are a con artist.

9) If the car has 5% tinted windows, they most likely are a con artist who didn't care for the car. It might be hard to sell it to the average person if you buy it and become the seller.

10) If the title of their advertisement is unusually long, then they are a con artist.

11) If their pictures are in a city that looks run down and very shady, then they are a con artist.

12) If you see the same car being advertised at the top of the list every day or two, then they are a con artist.

13) Advice to the more experienced private party car seller: Some con artists might "badge" a car to make it seem like the value is much greater than it really is. For example, a base model fifth generation Chevrolet Camaro is a 1LT. It comes standard with cloth seats and 16 inch rims. Many folks will buy used 2LT RS rims, leather seat upgrades and RS "badge" stickers, and sell it for $6,000 more than it is really worth. Again, con artists.

Autotrader

Autotrader.com is a better internet site to find deals that cars.com and cargurus.com because all advertisements must be paid for. While the dollar amount will vary based on things like the amount of pictures you use, the length of time you post it, and paying for a featured listing, the advertiser has to pay for it, nonetheless. The reason that is an advantage to you as the buyer is because the seller is investing money into the advertisement. That generally means that they are not flipping cars. Car flippers and car dealers will use free advertising almost 100% of the time because they are trying to move cars quickly. However, there are exceptions. From time to time, dealers and flippers will pay for a small advertisement, but they are still pretty easy to identify. Use the strategies outlined in the Craigslist section above to identify the con artists.

Autotrader works the same way as Craigslist. You will pull up the website, click on the advanced search option, then coordinate your search the same way you would outlined in the Craigslist section above.

Cars.com
Cars.com is a great website to locate cars as well, but cars.com will allow the seller to post a free 30 day advertisement at no cost, as long as they only use five pictures. This is obviously a good way to weed out the con artists. If the advertisement only has five pictures, and it is written similar to the section in Craigslist, then I would recommend moving on to the next opportunity.

Facebook Marketplace
Facebook Marketplace is an interesting buying site. There are pros and cons to marketplace. Here are some of the basics that I would recommend looking for:

1) You can look at the seller's profile after you've read their advertisement. This is a good thing, because you can figure out if they are using a real or fake profile. If the profile doesn't have pictures of them, then I would recommend flagging it as a con artist. If the profile shows pictures of many cars, then they should be flagged as a con artist as well. They are most likely flipping for profit. If they are selling 20 other cars under their profile, then they most definitely are car flippers. If the profile shows a mother of two kids, photos of a recent trip

to Disney World, and someone who posts regularly about their daughter's lacrosse games, then that is someone you want to consider purchasing a car from.

2) You can look at the number of views compared to when they originally posted the advertisement. If the advertisement has been up for only two hours, it has had 375 views and you've determined through your KBB pricing tutorial that it is a great deal, then you'll want to message them quickly and have a conversation.

3) You can select a distance as a specific diameter in miles to the location you'd like to target. Depending on where you live, you may need to extend your distance to cover more potential cars.

4) One of the disadvantages to Facebook marketplace is that you can only private message the seller. In the event that you found what looks to be a great deal, I would recommend messaging them and asking them for the best phone number and time to call them as opposed to texting everything on messenger.

3.3 – Carfax Reports

When buying a used car, there are way more scam artists trying to turn a profit then there are good people trying to sell good cars. My objective within this manual is to teach you how to both buy and sell good cars so all parties, whether buyer or seller, will walk away feeling like a winner. One of the ways to accomplish this is to balance the opportunity to make a profit with maintaining your integrity and reputation when selling the car you own. One

ne fundamental ways to ensure that you are not compromising your integrity is to sell cars to people without any issues (mitigating risk). The best way to ensure that the cars you buy do not have any issues are the following:
1) Speak with the mechanic and/or dealership that serviced the vehicle you want to buy
2) Review all the maintenance records from the seller you are buying the car from
3) Purchase and review a Carfax report

The Carfax report is by far the best vehicle history report on the market. It will provide a great amount of data. Data which will help you determine whether or not the car is a good deal or not. Here is a list of the important data that a Carfax report will provide:
1) The Vehicle Identification Number (VIN)
2) The year, make and model of the car
3) The engine
4) The drivetrain
5) Accident history
6) Damage history
7) Number of owners
8) Type of ownership (personal, rental or corporate)
9) Last reported odometer reading
10) Dates of all maintenance performed
11) Dealership and/or mechanic who performed the work
12) Comments regarding the service (oil/filter chance, new tires and alignment, etc)

13) Carfax History Based Value (an independent retail and trade-in value based on the information contained in the VIN)

Carfax has been known to not always have everything reported, such as accidents, certain maintenance performed, etc. However, the Carfax report will typically give the most accurate information of all its competitors. Without the evidence of maintenance records that were kept by the previous owner(s), the Carfax report is the next best thing to ensure the integrity of the vehicle. Carfax reports are a great resource. I would recommend purchasing one for every car that you are going to buy. There are two reasons I would recommend it. First, the Carfax report should provide any issues such as accidents, multiple owners, odometer tampering, etc. Second, the Carfax report typically will provide a retail value of $1,500 to $2,000 over the excellent value on KBB. This is a great selling tool as it evidences that the car you are going to sell is valued much higher on the Carfax report than what you bought it for under the KBB fair value.

3.4 – Know the Seller before you meet the Seller

Would you rather buy a car from a 72 year old female retired teacher or a 19 year old high school graduate who currently works part time at Popeye's chicken? Nothing against the dude at Popeye's. I used to work at a fast food chicken joint when I was in high school. So nothing but love. However with respect, I'd rather buy a car from the former than the latter. That's just me. Either way, when you are purchasing a car from a private party seller, you never quite know who is selling the car until you meet them. Or could you? If it is my desire to meet a potential seller face to face, then I typically like to know who I am meeting before I even get in my car.

This leads us to our next topic, knowing the seller before you meet the seller. The internet is a wonderful tool when gathering information about a seller. If you can ascertain the seller's first and last name, their city and state and/or zip code, then you typically can research a ton of information about them. Some would call this creepy. I would call it intelligent. Let's say I found that good old 2010 Honda Accord LX-P in a car buying search. You remember, the same one we used in our KBB example. Let's assume he was advertising his car on Craigslist Raleigh (North Carolina). His asking price was $7,200, which was equal to the Good value on KBB. He is the original owner. He provided his full name in the Craigslist advertisement as Henry Ford. He also provided his zip code as 27513. I would recommend starting to research him by his name and address.

White Pages
Whitepages.com is an excellent resource to find out more about where someone lives. Some of the advantages of white pages is that searches are free to the public. Often times, we can use the data to ensure that the address the seller provides us is accurate and matches to them. Other times, we can use a name and zip code search to learn where the seller lives so we can investigate the value of the home they live in.

Here are the steps to research someone on white pages:
1) Open whitepages.com
2) Enter the seller's name and zip code
3) Once the search displays, select the individual that you believe to be the seller. This might take a few tries. You may even need to have a conversation with them prior to confirming that you have the right information.
4) Once you've determined their identity, you can at least understand the age demographic of who you are buying the car from.

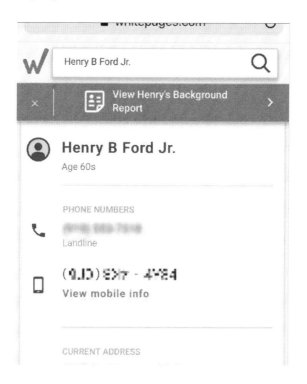

Zillow.com
Now that you've identified your seller, I would recommend researching their property value. To put this all in context of why you are doing it, consider this question. Who do you

think you are going to negotiate a better deal with for a 2010 Honda Accord LX-P with 100,000 miles on it?

1) A 64 year old retired school teacher who just bought his wife a brand new Jeep Cherokee Limited. They live in a house near Raleigh, NC valued at $764,000, which they bought 19 years ago for $374,000.
2) A 19 year old high school graduate who lives at home with his mom and dad. His reason for selling is that he has too many cars in his driveway and needs to part with a few of them.

The retired guy listed above probably just wants to make a quick sale and move on, because he doesn't need the money. He practically owns his home outright and just bought his wife a brand new $48,000 car off the lot. He doesn't need to haggle over $800. This is why researching the value of his house ahead of time can put you in a position of knowing your seller before you even meet him.

Here is how you research his property:
1) Log on to Zillow.com
2) Type in the address that you researched on whitepages
3) Once you've located their address on Zillow, then start analyzing your data
4) This should be your dream seller. I would highly recommend looking for these people as your target sellers.

53   Dr,
Raleigh, NC 27613

4 beds · 4 baths · 4,280 sqft

● FOR SALE

$735,000

Zestimate: $739,132

Est. Mortgage: $2,938/mo

Get pre-qualified

🚗 __ min

Facebook and LinkedIn

Facebook and LinkedIn are two fantastic social media sites to consider using once you've identified your seller's address and value of their home. 85+% of the time, you will be able to locate the seller on these websites. This is all part of your data and information gathering. Using these websites should be able to provide you some context regarding who you are purchasing the car from. Once you find them online, I would recommend painting the picture of the seller's lifestyle:

1) Marriage status

2) Children status
3) Employment status
4) Career title (LinkedIn)
5) Length of employment (LinkedIn)
6) Hobbies
7) Interests
8) Political opinion
9) Religious viewpoint

Once you've collected all your data on the seller, now it's time to think about the psychology of what the conversation might be about. Go back to the example of the 64 year old retired teacher versus the 19 year old high school graduate. I would recommend asking these questions to yourself before you have a conversation with the seller:
1) How can I get them to like me instantly?
2) What would I have to say to them to have them sell the car to me instead of someone else?
3) Will they be offended if I ask specific questions about the maintenance history of their car?
4) If they asked me why I am looking to buy the car, what would I tell them?

3.5 - The Art of the Deal: Negotiation as the Buyer

Now that we have learned how to both research car values and identify deals on the internet, the next step is to tie it all together and negotiate the deal as the buyer. There are six important things to remember if we are negotiating a deal as the buyer, in order of importance:

1) The buyer is always in the driver's seat (no pun intended). Cash is king. The car is not the king. This means that the buyer always has the upper hand, no matter what. Even when the demand for a car is high and the supply for the car is low, the buyer will still always have the advantage.
2) People sell things to people they like.
3) Prior to the negotiation, always research and determine your ceiling amount. Never exceed this amount within your negotiation.
4) Understand that you are never wrong to walk away from a deal. No matter how wonderful, sexy and profitable you think the deal could be, there will be always be others if this one does not work out.
5) Go with your gut instinct. If your gut tells you to walk away, then do it. If your gut tells you to offer cash and close the deal immediately, then proceed with caution to the steps to get you to finalize the deal.
6) Learn something from every single purchase, and write it down.

I've reviewed a few of my competitor's car buying and selling manuals. While a few of them make some valid points, I noticed a great amount of opportunity for them to explain the psychology of the sale. People buy things from people they like. If someone doesn't like you, then they are not going to sell a car to you. Here are the lessons you will need to be a successful negotiator.

Lesson # 1. Be nice. Don't be an asshole. This is business. While you are not the seller's best friend, there are little things that you can do that will go a long way. Remember the guy standing in the middle of the football field? Let's pretend he's the seller. Remember all the people in the NFL stadium stands? Let's pretend that is you along with 50,000 other potential buyers. Let's also pretend that he is selling the 2010 Honda Accord LX-P. Let's say the seller is asking $6,800, which is only $100 over the KBB fair value of the car. Let's say he wrote that he was the original owner on his Craigslist advertisement, and that he has every maintenance record available since he drove it off the lot in 2010. You and every other potential buyer are reading this advertisement knowing that you could buy it and make a $2,500 profit within two weeks.

So here is the million dollar question. What is it that you can do to get him to sell you the car and not someone else?

Step one is to figure out a way to have a conversation over the phone rather than through a text message. You could start by texting the phone number, introducing yourself by providing your first name, explaining that you are looking for a third vehicle for the winter, and you would like to know what the best time to call him would be. Once he responds and tells you the best time to call, then make every effort to call him within five minutes after he told you. Even if he doesn't answer and you have to leave a message, it at least shows that you are very interested in the car and you made an attempt to call him when he asked. This is part of being nice. People like people that are nice.

Step two is to have an intelligent conversation with the seller. This is where all that proactive research you

previously did will pay off. Organize a flow of
that make sense, are to the point and will not
time. I would recommend asking these op
questions in order and applicable to the car:

1) Are you the original owner? (you only ask this if you are unsure)
2) If not, then how long have you owned the car for? (based on the answer, you know if you are dealing with a flipper or someone who cared for the car)
3) What is the date on the title when you took ownership of the car?
4) Whose name is on the title?
5) Is there more than one person's name on the title?
6) If yes, then what is their relationship?
7) Why are you selling it?
8) How far back do you have maintenance receipts?
9) What major services have you had completed personally while you owned the car? For example, automatic transmission fluid flushes, timing belt changes, tires and brakes replaced?
10) Has the car ever been in an accident?
11) How many miles are on the tires?
12) Is there any rust or frame damage?
13) Does the car have air conditioning?
14) What specific model is your car?
15) Did it come with any specific appearance and/or performance packages?
16) Is the car stock, or were there any performance modifications made to the car?

Once you've asked most or all these questions, the seller will know you are serious about his car. I would highly mmend acting as if his car is at the top of your list of the cars you've been looking at. Make him feel special about his car. Let him feel as though you are the right buyer for his car. Most of my competitors would encourage you tell the seller that you are looking at other cars that are cheaper, so he will need to lower his price to keep in line with them. I would say not to do that. No one wants to hear that as a seller. It is insulting. You are being an asshole when you don't need to be one. Make the deal about you and the seller only. Do not suggest that you can buy a car from another guy down the street. You both know you can do that. You both also know that he can sell it to someone else down the street. You want to give the seller a reason to put you at the top of his list to come look at his car. If it is a great deal, then the seller is being contacted by many other people than just you. So make sure you are at the top of his list of people to come see it. Set up a time and place to meet. Make sure you've thought about your personal schedule prior to asking him when you can come see it. Try your best to meet his availability. I would recommend proactively providing two or three days and timeslots that work for you. Ask him if those times work in his schedule. Make sure that you set up a time and place to meet before you get off the phone with him. If for any reason you are unable to make the original time and place you agreed upon, then call him back, let him know right away and set up a new time. Do not be a "no-show." It compromises your integrity, and everyone's time is valuable.

Step three is to negotiate your deal. Once you've met with the seller, the most important thing you can do is to have the $5,000 cash sitting in your front pocket, ready make a deal. Let's assume he is selling a 2012 Chevroiei Sonic LTZ hatchback with 48,000 miles for an asking price of $5,500. The KBB fair private party value is $5,200. You've determined that your ceiling for this particular car is $4,500 and no more. If you've done your homework, you've looked over the car, you've taken it for a test drive and you know you are going to buy the car, then it's time to assume the sale as the buyer. I'd recommend following this sales script. You will close the deal 90+% of the time.

"Greg, I really appreciate you giving me the opportunity to come look at your Chevy Sonic LTZ. Your car is exactly what I am looking for. I've had the opportunity to look at a few other cars over the last few weeks, but yours is absolutely the one I'd like to drive home. I can give you $4,300 cash today for your car. We can drive over to your local bank together and deposit the money right into your account if you'd like, just so your local bank can confirm the funds. Then, you can sign the title over to me right at the bank. I can come back to your house in a few hours with my wife/girlfriend/brother to pick up the car later today. Once I get the car home, I will get it registered and inspected at my local DMV tomorrow."

If he doesn't like your offer, he will counteroffer you. Maybe he says he won't take less than $5,000 for it. So tell him, you'd love to drive the car home today, so you will offer him $4,500. Most times he will agree to your counteroffer. However, if he says $4,800 or no deal, then this is how you respond:

"Greg, I can't thank you enough for letting me come see your car. I can only spend $4,500. This is what I budgeted for, considering I have to pay a few $100s in taxes, tags and titling. Let me think about your offer for a few days, but unfortunately for now I gave you my best offer of $4,500 cash, which I can give you today. I appreciate you letting me come to look at it."

Now, start to walk away. If he hasn't yelled to you from the top of his driveway to come back before you got to your car, then expect a phone call from him for you to return to his house after you've already left to make the deal. Remember, the buyer always has the upper hand. He wants to sell that car to you much worse than you want to buy the car from him. This is the art of the deal. If for whatever reason you've haggled over $200 over your ceiling amount, then it simply was not meant to be. There will be other deals. You are never wrong to walk away from a deal. There will be others. Always.

As a percentage, the baby boomer generation (50 to 75 years old) tends to be the best generation to purchase a car from. For the most part, retired folks are the most honest and the most eager to sell to a person they like. They would rather talk to someone over the phone than have a conversation over a text message. These are great folks to target when you are buying. The art of finding and buying a car is analogous to finding a date on match.com. You need to weed through all the bull before you find the one you want to land.

3.6 - The Art of the Deal: Negotiation as the Seller

Now that we have learned to how to research car values, identify deals on the internet, and negotiate a deal as a buyer, the next step is to learn how to negotiate the deal as the seller. There are important things to remember if we are negotiating a deal as the seller, in order of importance:

1) There is always a buyer. You just have to find them.
2) If you can get the potential buyer to pull up in your driveway to look at your car, then chances are you will sell it.
3) If you've detailed the car to make it look like it's right off the showroom floor when they show up, then chances are you will sell it.
4) If you are a great storyteller, then chances are you will sell it.
5) If you've advertised your car online efficiently, then your car will sell itself (more to come on this in the advertising and marketing section of the manual).
6) People buy things from people they like.
7) Prior to the negotiation, always research and determine your bottom line acceptance amount. Never drop below this amount within your negotiation.
8) Understand that you are never wrong to tell someone no to their face. No matter how difficult it may seem, you eventually will sell it.
9) Learn something from every single sale, and write it down.

Back to my competitors for a moment. Many of them suggest telling buyers that you have other buyers who want to buy your car. They'll recommend saying something like, "if you don't make me an offer today, then already I have two other people lined up that already made me an offer." No one wants to hear that. It's a turn off. The buyer will not like you. Nor should he. You're being an asshole. Let your relationship with your buyer just be between the two of you. Have tunnel vision with that buyer while you are talking with them. Don't bring others into it. This transaction is between you and the guy standing in front and no one else. So keep it that way. Contrary to my competitors who are charging you money to teach you how to buy and sell cars their way, I would recommend using my approach. You will close more sales this way. Make them feel like they are the right fit for your car. Let them feel as though you like them so much, that they are at the top of your list of who you want to sell it to. People will buy from people they like.

Whether you sell your car to the first person that comes to see your car or the fourth, there will always be a buyer. Some cars may take longer to sell than others. Especially when you consider that your fundamental goal is to maximize your profit on every single car. If you are only selling four under your name and four under your spouse's/significant other's name, then you can flip eight per year and still appear like you are simply a car enthusiast to the DMV. That means you have about a month and a half to buy and sell each car, one at a time. There's no rush. If you want to flip 50 cars per month, then you need to research getting a dealer's license. That is not what I am teaching you in this manual. I am teaching you private party car sales only.

The first thing a potential buyer is going to do is contact you, expressing interest in your car. Let's go back to the 2010 Honda Accord LX-P with 100,000 miles. Let's say the private party KBB value is $8,360 in excellent value. You pulled a Carfax report on it when you originally purchased the car, and the Carfax retail value was listed as $9,740 for your VIN number. You advertised the Honda on Craigslist, cars.com and Facebook Marketplace. Two days after listing it on all the various advertising platforms, you receive a private message from Lorraine Graham at 6:30 am. She explains that she is a registered nurse who is working 8:00 am to 7:00 pm that day, but would like to come see your car the morning after.

Here is what I would recommend doing to prepare for her coming to see your Honda:
1) Clean your car. Nobody wants to see the dried up pollen and rain spots all over the exterior of your car. Nor do they want to see your five year old's Cheerios and car seat in the back seat since you've been using it the last three weeks to go back and forth to work. So give it a good wash, vacuum and even a quick wax if you have time. Spray the tires with a tire foam to give them that glossy look. Spray some car freshener or Febreze to make it smell good.

2) Pull up her Facebook profile and figure out who she is before she comes over. Use a little Psychology

101. If she reached out to you on Facebook, then you can quickly view her profile to see what she is all about. Let's assume you confirm on her profile that she is a registered nurse. Perhaps the profile says she lives in the city two towns over, which you know is a 40 minute drive. You notice that she has several pictures of her three granddaughters. You scroll through her posts and notice that 90% of her posts are of religious posts, where obviously her faith and family are important to her. This is the type of person I'd want coming to my house. She is wealthy. Registered Nurses make great money, so she can afford my car. She lives 40 minutes away, which means if she's willing to drive out to see my car, it's at least two hours out of her busy day. She's most likely not a criminal. You may laugh, but there are plenty of criminals out there. I wouldn't want one showing up on my doorstep. She most likely will not need a loan for this particular car, which means you can both close the deal quickly if you negotiate the right way.

3) Have a good story as to why you are selling the car ahead of time. Become a storyteller. If she asks you why you are selling your car (which she should), you should be able to explain why you've only owned the car for three weeks without sounding like a con artist. I'd recommend saying that your grandparent recently passed away, and that you inherited the car as part of the trust. You've determined that you really don't need the car, so you'd like to sell it and take your family to Disney World with the money.

Does it really matter what the story is? No. As long as you are selling her a good car, then everybody wins. There are other stories that you can make up, but this one seems to work best.

NOTE: For the more experienced car sellers, I'd recommend whiting out all the personal information on the previous owner's maintenance receipts, then photo copying them. This way the next owner will have access to previous maintenance history, but they will not easily be able to contact the previous owner to verify your story. You don't need people coming back to your house after you've sold the car.

4) Clean up your house, mow your lawn, take a shower and put on some nice clothes before she gets there. As ridiculous as this might sound, it works. Again, people buy things from people they like. Regardless of the fact that you've only owned the car for three weeks, you are setting a first impression that she is buying a car from a clean, responsible person who takes pride in all their belongings.

If she physically comes out to your house, then this is a good indication that she will have already made up her mind to buy your car. Therefore, confirm her decision as she is pulling into the driveway. Her heart is going to be pounding. She is going to be both nervous and excited. Have all your others cars (if applicable) in the garage. That Honda should be on the street, right out in front of your house, looking like it's right off the showroom floor. Once she drives up and parks, don't come outside yet. Give her an opportunity to look at the car for a few minutes. This will build her excitement. Once she comes to the door, greet her by making sure you say her name. Tell her you're glad she took the time to come see your car, and thank her for making the time. This small statement will validate that you are a good person in her mind. She wants to buy a car from someone she likes.

Now, show her your car. Point out the features and show her how things work. Ask her to stand in front and in back of the car while you step on the brake lights to prove that they work. Offer to try the air conditioner for her (assuming it works well) while you are on your test drive with her. Stick to the things that make the car attractive to a buyer. Open the hood for her. Point out the fluids, and tell her you recently had it inspected (if you had). This will show her that you took responsibility to complete your due diligence in making sure the car is running well.

Closing the Sale
You've already made all your money on the purchase price of your car. You've decided your bottom line, and you know you will not take less than that. I've you've followed all the steps that I've outlined above, then expect to receive an offer for about $300 to $500 less than your asking price. If this is the case, and the amount is above your bottom line, then counteroffer a few $100s more by meeting half way between your asking price and her offer. Offer to not only land at that half way point, but complete a Bill of Sale which is perhaps $2,000 less than your asking price. This way, she will not have to pay as much in transfer taxes, and your selling price will look as though it is much closer to

what you originally purchased the car for. It is a win/win for both of you. If it is considerably lower, then flat out say no to the offer. Tell them you appreciate them coming out, but you will not be willing to go under $X.00 (your bottom line amount plus $300). This way, if they counteroffer your "bottom line," then you can squeeze out an additional $300 if they drive away and you want to call them back to actually sell it for your bottom line amount.

Chapter Four

How to Inspect the Car Prior to the Purchase

Our fundamental goal of the manual is to maximize our profit on buying and selling cars while also mitigating risk associated with the cars we want to buy. One of our secondary goals is to buy and sell cars that need little to no maintenance and/or repairs so we can maximize those profit margins. Therefore, ensuring that we are buying a good car to eventually sell is paramount to the process. It is easy to get excited about a deal that we find on the internet. But pictures and descriptions can only go so far. Let's go back to the 2010 Honda Accord LX-P with 100,000 miles. Let's assume we've done our homework, we know the seller is in the ballpark with their asking price, we've contacted the seller and we arrived at his house. Here are the things that I would recommend looking for as you inspect the car:

Exterior
1) Exterior/Body/Frame: Evaluate the body thoroughly. Search for dents, scratches, sun damage (paint fading), paint peeling, scuffed or dented bumpers and fenders.
2) Compare body panels for color inconsistencies. For example, look at the front driver's side fender. Ensure that the paint looks exactly the same as the driver's side door right next to it.
3) Check moldings and under the wheel wells for overspray. Often times when a car has been in an accident, the body mechanic can never be absolutely perfect when they paint certain spots of the car. This is especially obvious

within the wheel wells. The Carfax report may not always show that the car has been in an accident. So this is where completing your extra due diligence becomes important.

4) Open the hood and look at the fluids. The engine coolant should have a nice color to it and not look cloudy or dark. This would be indicative of needing to be changed. Also, check the radiator support. This is the metal frame that holds the radiator in place. Ensure it is not dented or damaged. Sometimes you will notice the car has been painted after evaluating this.

5) Check for rust. Surface rust is typically acceptable to some degree depending on the age of the car. However, if you can stick a pen through the frame, then walk away from the car.

6) Overspray on plastic parts or fender wells.

7) Look in the trunk. Check the spare tire and trunk pan to ensure there is no water damage or smells such as mildew.

8) Check all door hinges to ensure they are not rusty or broken.

Interior

1) Take a look at the cloth or leather seat upholstery. Ensure it's not so dirty that a you cannot clean it.

2) Check mechanical buttons and switches, such as power windows, power door locks, power seats, radio controls, Bluetooth, etc.

3) Check engine lights and/or other warning lights on the dashboard. The O2 oxygen sensor typically fails after 50,000 to 75,000 miles. This will make the check engine light appear. The sensor is attached to either the exhaust manifold or the catalytic converter. The sensor ensures the right gas and oil mixture is happening. This

is a very common engine problem and typically costs in excess of $500 to replace.
4) Ensure all doors open from inside and out.
5) Ensure the air conditioner and heater work properly.

Suspension
1) Suspension and braking system: Walk around each of the four corners of the car. Push down on each corner. If the car bounces more than 2 or 3 times, then this is an indication that the shocks need to be replaced. A good shock or strut will absorb any bounce. Good shocks will cease bouncing after only 1 bounce. A soft and bouncy ride means typically means you will need new struts and shocks.
2) Check timing belts for proper tightness. If you hear squealing, this is typically an indication that the timing belt needs to be replaced.
3) Check tire ware and deflation in tires. A good habit to get into is to take a penny with you. If you put the penny in the tread and part of Abe Lincoln's head is missing, then your tires most likely need replacing.
4) Look around the valve cover gasket, power steering fluid, brake fluid and engine coolant reservoirs for excessive leakage.
5) When checking the oil, make sure that the oil is not a milky color. Milky oil means that you may have an internal water leak in your engine, caused by a blown head gasket or a cracked head. That is one of the most expensive repairs you will come across.
6) Transmission oil should have the same color (RED) as most power steering fluid.
7) Black oil (uncared for car) may result in a slight noise/knocking in the engine.
8) Check the air conditioning to ensure it works.

Take a test drive
1) Listen for vehicle noises. Close the windows. Drive with them open. Do not to let the seller distract you from listening to sounds the car could be making.
2) With the car running and in park, check the steering. Turn the wheel from left to right. If the wheel squeaks or grinds when turning, you should know that you may be low on power steering fluid. You may have a problem with the power steering pump or rack and pinion steering.
3) Check the alignment by noticing banging in the steering wheel, or the car pulling to one side or the other during the test drive. Alignment issues typically could include worn ball joints, tie rods, misaligned camber or toe alignments. These repairs can be costly, so you might consider a professional inspection be completed prior to purchasing the car.
4) Check for fluid leaks after the test drive. NOTE: If the air conditioner has been running, then the water condensation under the car would only be from that. There would be no need to be alarmed with that. Greasy, black oil dripping would be a major concern. Also, colored fluid (reds, greens and blues) might be indicative of power steering fluid or engine coolant leaks.
9) Check the brakes by listening to squealing or rubbing. About 60% of your braking comes from your front wheels.
5) Listen for loud engine noises such as knocking. This means serious issues and it would be better to walk away.

After you've completed your inspection, if you still are in doubt, then ask the seller if you can take the car to an independent auto mechanic of your choice. The mechanic will typically charge from $30 to $100 to look the car over and ensure a good bill of health prior to purchasing it. If they refuse, then they are hiding something so walk away. Most private party sellers with a conscience and good reputation will allow you to take it to a mechanic if you ask them.

When discussing flaws with the car, I'd recommend doing it diplomatically. Many car salesmen will tell you to point out every little negative detail of the car. I would say it is a very bad idea to do that. Why? Because you're being an asshole. This is a several year old car. If you were buying a car that came off the showroom floor brand new, then that's a different story. But you are not. It is a used car, owned by a private party seller. They know it has dings and dents. They know the air conditioner doesn't run as ice cold as it did eight years ago. They get it. So here is how I would encourage you to go about the conversation, assuming that you still want to maximize getting the best deal:

"John, it looks like you've taken really good car of your car. It's exactly what I'm looking for. It has a few dents and scratches here and there, and the air conditioner is not quite ice cold, but due to the way you've cared for it, those things are not really a big deal to me. I really like your car."

Chapter Five

Advertising your Car

This is arguably going to be one of my favorite chapters to write. The reason being is because your car can sell itself with great advertising. There are a few questions that you should always ask yourself as you are creating your advertisement to sell your car. If you were a potential buyer looking at advertisements, ask yourself the following questions:

1) Who would I be looking to buy a car from?
2) What would I want to see that would stop me and grab my attention?
3) When is the best time for me to look for cars?
4) Where would I look for a car?

Let's paint a picture of a prospective buyer in the market. This is a good example, because it happens all the time. Let's assume I am a potential buyer searching for a used car. I know I don't want to buy a brand new car. Let's assume I am a 45 year old father of two girls who are ages 16 and 14 respectively. My 16 year old daughter just got her driver's license. My wife and I determined that our lives would be so much easier if we bought her a car to get back and forth to school, lacrosse practice and her part time job at Rita's Water Ice on the weekends. Our daughter gets very good grades, she is a starter on the JV lacrosse team and she earns about $150 a week at the water ice shop where she has worked consistently for 3 months. We feel she earned our help in buying a car to get around town. We know the car doesn't need to be fancy. We've budgeted for $6,000 cash, as we felt that would provide a stable and economical vehicle that will not break down nor have significant mechanical problems in the short term. We'd like to buy a car with 80,000 to 100,000 miles, as we feel the car might need too much work if we search for cars with over 150,000 miles. We want to buy her a four cylinder engine, front drive, automatic transmission car. The car doesn't need to have leather seats or a 20 inch wheel package. It is her starter vehicle and our "added quality of life" vehicle. We will look to purchase a car that is great on gas, because we know we will be filling the tank for her often.

Who am I looking to buy a car from?
Someone like me or older. I want to purchase a car from an original owner, if possible. I want to buy a car from someone who can show me all the maintenance records to evidence it has been taken care of. I want to ensure the current owner has had it inspected, and that the inspection stickers are not expired. I want to buy a car from someone who lives in a nice community if I need to drive to their house.   Therefore, when I start searching for cars online, I am going to view the description on cars that I perceive as fitting that scenario.

Who am I avoiding?
Scam artists. I'm not comfortable taking my 16 year old to someone's address where the background pictures in the ad look like an abandoned warehouse that was used in one of the Saw movies. I want to avoid the guy that is stupid enough to advertise his car in his "buy here pay here" car

dealership next to his 15 other cars while advertising in the "private seller" section.

What would I want to see that would stop me and grab my attention?
Considering that 95+% of car buyers are starting and continuing their search for a used car online, I have to ensure that my car's profile picture stands out over everyone else's. So how do I do that, considering that there are so many pictures of cars that look the same? Ensure that you have covered the following:

1) Take a picture at a public school on a grassy field, where there are nothing but baseball and soccer fields in the background. You might also consider taking a picture in your driveway or outside your house. However, this should be a backup plan to the school. Any pictures you take with something in the background that would distract your potential buyer and take your eyes off your car will do just that. Your primary goal in online advertising is to make the potential buyer stop when they get to your car. That $\frac{1}{2}$ a second pause of a private buyer's reaction time can either sell your car or not.

2) Make sure your car looks like it's right off the showroom floor. Your car should be washed, waxed, interior vacuumed, engine wiped down and tires glossed. Your initial photo is the only photo potential buyers will see at first, until they decide to open your advertisement. Therefore, you will want your car to stand out.

3) Using your cell phone, take a picture sitting down at the front driver's side of your car, and take the picture on an angle. You will want to capture the front bumper, the hood, the roof, the side doors and the tires all in one picture. You should take your pictures on a sunny day. You should take several pictures at several different angles so when you get home, you can choose the one that was best.

4) Take 100 different pictures of your car. Take pictures at all different angles. Get pictures of your interior by opening the sunroof (if applicable) and doors as to expose added sunlight. When taking pictures of your dashboard and interior, slide the front seats all the way back as to create an illusion that there is more room then there actually is. Do the same thing when taking photos of the rear seats by sliding the front seats all the way up as far as they can go. Take pictures of the engine. If the fluids are colorful and in good shape, take specific photos of that as to indicate you are someone who takes exceptional care of your car. Take pictures of the tire tread. If the tires are new or almost new, then take a penny and rest it in the tread to prove that the new owner will not need to replace them for quite some time. Take pictures of the sunroof (if applicable) and the radio. These are added features that make your car stand out. Take pictures of the trunk and even the spare tire.

5) Take pictures of all your maintenance records, books, two sets of car keys and original window sticker (when applicable) that came with the car. I would recommend whiting out the personal

information on all the maintenance receipts you have, even if they were from the previous owner before you.

6) Take a picture of the KBB value and/or the Carfax retail value when the value is close to or above your asking price. This will provide evidence that you've done your homework and you are asking for a purchase amount that is justified.

7) Once you've taken all your pictures, open two apps on your phone called Aviary and Pic Collage. You can use Aviary to blur license plates and crop photos. You can use Pic Collage to create a 4 in 1 picture at all different angles, since some online advertising sites will limit the amount of pictures that you can upload.

The goal of your photos is to get the prospective buyer to see as many different pictures of your car as they can at all different angles. You are aiming to have them almost see your car in 3D as if they are looking at it in person.

The importance of the vehicle description

The description of your vehicle that you provide to your potential buyer is paramount to your sales objective. Again, your car can sell itself if you advertise it efficiently compared to your competitors. Think about it. You are not physically standing in front of the buyer and telling them about your car when they are searching online. This is why the vehicle description is so important. Back in the 80s, our parents would purchase a three line advertisement in the Classified section of our local newspaper. It would typically read, "1985 Pontiac Fiero, 5spd, 4 cyl, red, 100k mi." There were no pictures. It cost them about $25 to run an advertisement for three weeks with that many characters. Once they started exceeding those characters, the ad costed more money. The world we live in now allows you to advertise your car with as many as 1,000 total characters. This provides you a significant advantage over prior generations. Writing a detailed vehicle description separates the successful from the unsuccessful. Here is a blueprint that you can follow when writing a detailed and educated vehicle description:

2010 Honda Accord LX-P
Private owner with car title
Garage kept
4 cylinder engine
34 highway miles per gallon
Front wheel drive
100,000 miles
Automatic transmission
Alloy wheels

Black exterior/tan interior
Power driver's seat
Air conditioning
Maintenance receipts
Owner's manuals
Original window sticker
Both sets of car keys with alarm features
Recently completed maintenance included an oil and filter change, tire rotation and new battery
Recently purchased Carfax report proving no prior accidents
Please call or text the cell phone number provided for more information

This information provided is factual. It is also brief and to the point. When the potential buyer sees your advertisement and opens it, you have less than one minute to provide them what I call a WOW factor. There is no need to tell them why you are selling it in your vehicle description. If you did your job and gave them good information and good pictures, then they are going to call or text you for more information, which is what you want them to do anyway. You want to leave about 10% of the car to their imagination. Think about an attractive woman on the beach. You like to daydream about what's under the 10% of clothing on her body that is covering her up.

If you follow these steps, then you will have a much greater chance of having someone both call you and then coming to see your car in person. If you did a superior job with your car advertisement, then you most likely have sold the car even prior to the buyer coming to see it in person.

When is the best time for me to come look at cars?

When am I available? Most, but not all people have full time jobs. At least the ones that can afford to pay for your car in cash. Therefore, considering the timing of when you post your advertisements can have an impact on the success of potential buyers actually seeing your ad. Take Facebook local group sites for example. Let's assume I requested to be added to the Raleigh NC buy, sell and trade group page. I should aim to list my advertisement at 8:00 am on a Saturday morning. This is generally the time that buyers that I want to see my ad are waking up and starting their weekend. Typically, before they get out of bed, they look at their phone for about 15 or 20 minutes to see what's good in the world at the time. Another good time is around 8:30 pm when people are laying down to turn off their brain before bed.

Regarding Craigslist and other online sites like cars.com and autotrader.com, a good rule of thumb is to create a new listing closer to the weekend, as this is the time that potential buyers will usually start looking harder.

Where would I look for a car?

If I am a basic private party car buyer and not a car flipper, I am not thinking about every possible internet website available to me. I'm only thinking about a handful of the popular ones that will give me the most bang for my buck in a search. I am also thinking about a 50 mile range maximum. I would highly prefer to buy a car in my own home state if possible. Cars.com, autotrader.com, Craigslist and Facebook Marketplace are really the only websites that I'm going to focus on. These are the websites that I would recommend focusing on as well when you are the private party seller. I would also recommend frequenting these sites to see how these other guys are marketing their cars. This way you can figure out what to do, what not to do and how to separate yourself from your online competitors.

Chapter 6

Identifying the forms associated with your title transfer and how to fill them out properly

There are really only two forms that hold significant importance to the private party car buying and selling process. They are the car title and the bill of sale.

The car title
Many folks may get intimidated with the car title transfer. It can be an uncomfortable process if either you don't know how to fill it out or you don't have a state auto notary to expedite the process for you. It is actually very simple. However, there are sticky points and red flags that you must be aware of regarding the title. So let's take each section one by one.

A "clean" title (or "clear" title)
When a title is referred to as "clean," it simply means that the car does not have any liens (money owed to a bank) has never been registered as a salvage, "R title" or total loss vehicle. A salvage title is issued by states when the vehicle has experienced damage caused by an unrepairable accident, flood or theft. When one of these scenarios occur, the insurance company will evaluate the cost to fix the vehicle. If the total cost to repair the vehicle are in excess of the value of the car, then the insurance company will issue a "salvage" title, therefore confirming the car a total loss.

The goal of this manual is to provide you quality information regarding the purchase and selling of cars in the private party market. Therefore, we won't even spend any more time discussing the bad titles. Just know that I would highly recommend buying and selling cars with a clean title. Here is a picture of a "clean" title versus a "salvage" title:

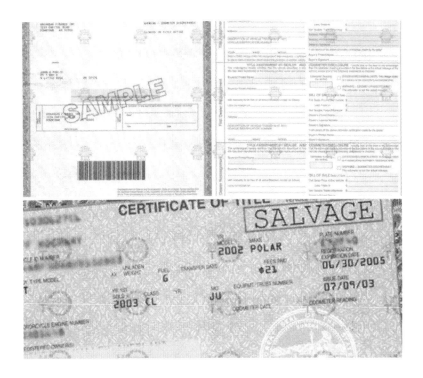

Filling out the car title for transfer

Depending on the state in which you reside, you and the buyer/seller may be required to transfer the title in person at a local Department of Motor Vehicles (DMV). You may also be required to transfer the title at a local auto notary. Again, this will depend on the state in which you reside. I would highly recommend going to the DMV or auto notary, as required by your state.

Certain states will permit you to sign over your title at your residence, then the buyer would take the title to the DMV or auto notary at a later date. While this is typically a normal practice for many car buyers and sellers, I wouldn't recommend it. If you are the seller and you sign your title over to a buyer, then you have no way of knowing how long it will take them to title your car, assuming they were truly planning on getting it titled to begin with. This can cause major headaches down the road. If the buyer drives your car home, never gets the title transferred into their name and gets in an accident three weeks later, then the DMV is going to get you involved again. It's just better to avoid all this potential mess by going to the DMV or auto notary and let them complete it on your behalf as an authorized government motor vehicle establishment.

The information you will need to fill out within the title is quite simple.
1) As a seller, you must sign and date as the registered owner.
2) Next, put the exact mileage. Do not leave blank or round up to the nearest 100 miles.
3) As a buyer, sign the section applicable to the buyer.
4) The seller will detach the perforated section (smaller section) and mail it into the DMV for processing.
5) The buyer will take the other section (the larger title section) and provide that to the DMV when they take it to the DMV to get it registered.

Bill of Sale

The bill of sale is synonymous with your sales receipt. This is the evidence of you both agreeing to the purchase/sale of the car. Just like the title, you will provide evidence of the date, time, mileage, year/make/model, and any specifics of what was agreed to. For example, the seller is selling the car "as is," or perhaps the seller agreed to offer a one month warranty up to $300 if the brakes failed inspection. This should all be agreed upon as part of the negotiation. The bill of sale will provide the specifics of the agreement, if there were any. It will also provide evidence of the date and time that the sale took place. Here is an example of a generic bill of sale document:

Chapter 7

Private party sellers versus licensed car dealers or wholesalers

Let's take the time to define each of these. A private party buyer/seller is someone who buys a car from either another private party seller or a car dealer. They are required to get the car registered and inspected in their name. They may use the car for a long period of time before they decide to sell it, trade it into a dealer or donate the car to a charity. From time to time, private party sellers will buy a car and sell it within a very short period of time. Some may even sell it with the hopes of making a profit. A dealer is someone who buys and sells cars, solely with the goal of earning a profit. The dealer is required to get a dealer's license. The wholesaler is required to only buy and sell cars from other dealers. They do not have the ability to purchase from a dealer and sell to the general public per their licensing agreement. There are several steps involved in obtaining a dealer's license. These include but are not limited to the following:

1) Leasing, renting or owning a building which contains at least two parking spaces and a full handicapped-accessible bathroom with sink and toilet
2) Taking courses to become a licensed car dealer
3) Paying up front registration fees
4) Taking classes that teach following a specific code of conduct and ethics according to state laws

5) Learning requirements regarding the accountability for vehicles that fall under Lemon Law criteria (mostly new cars)
6) Learning the requirements of local, state and federal government compliance regulations
7) Learning how wholesale dealers are only permitted to buy and sell to other car dealers. They are not permitted to buy and sell to the public

Typically there are pros and cons to being a private party buyer and seller. There are pros and cons to being a licensed car dealer or wholesaler. Let's explore each a bit further. My goal is to provide you the data you will need to decide the best path for you.

The Pros of being a private party buyer/seller
1) It requires no overhead or money up front except for a car to sell
2) There are minimal fees to advertise
3) There is no time limit on how fast you need to buy or sell a car
4) There (technically) may be no taxable requirement needed to be reported to the IRS
5) It can be a supplemental income to an existing full time job
6) You can use it as a personal vehicle for pleasure, commuting, etc until you sell it

The Cons of being a private party buyer/seller
1) You are limited in the amount of cars you can buy and sell per year according to the requirements of your state

2) If you get caught making substantial profit margins on multiple cars each year, then the DMV may require you to get a dealer's license
3) You are required to get each car titled, registered and inspected, which costs money

The Pros of being a car dealer or wholesaler
1) You are not limited in the amount of cars you can buy and sell per year
2) You can participate in dealer's auctions and purchase cars at auction price

The Cons of being a car dealer or wholesaler
1) There is a very large out of pocket start-up cost, typically above $50,000+
2) In most states, you are required to find a lot, get a bond, and have access to a physically handicapped accessible bathroom
3) You must take classes to prove you plan to operate with integrity
4) You most likely would need to spend a good amount of time creating a business plan to get approved for a loan
5) You will need to have your car dealer lot inspected both initially and continuously throughout the course of your ownership
6) You will be highly scrutinized by federal, state and local government entities to ensure adherence to applicable laws, policies, procedures and guidelines.
7) If you are unwilling and/or unable to get a dealer's license, then you may have to partner with a dealer.

Since I am writing this manual with my integrity in mind, then I won't elaborate on this.

Whether you decide to start in the private party car buying and selling world or immediately transition to getting a dealer's license, I would highly recommend earning some experience first. You shadow a car salesman, sell cars at a local dealership first, or have a mentor who can provide you some expertise, it is always good to have some experience prior to investing in cars to buy and sell for profit.

Remember, part of the fundamental goal of the manual is to mitigate risk while maximizing profit. Therefore, it is a best practice to learn how to find good deals that do not require significant repair costs. We want the profit to go into our business account, not the local mechanic's account. We also want to ensure we as private party car salesmen are not selling a car with known issues to someone else. That behavior destroys credibility and reputations.

Chapter 8

Philanthropy and Final Thought

I wrote this manual with my father in mind as I wrote it. Now that I am a father, I look back at my childhood and say to myself, "if I could be half the father that my father was to me, then I'll make a great Dad." I would have never got to where I am today, and have the passion for buying and selling cars today, if it weren't for him. He's owned quite a few awesome cars in his day. I plan to follow in his footsteps.

When I was 16 years old (almost 25 years ago), my Dad and I went to look at a red, 1985 Pontiac Fiero SE as our family's "third car." Yet, I knew my Dad was buying it primarily for me. I was the oldest of three boys, and my brothers were not of age yet. I had been hawking the local newspaper classified section every morning for two months with the anticipation of finding a somewhat reliable but fun sports car. When I came across the advertisement, I showed my Dad. He agreed that we should go see it. My Dad's plan was to take all $1,500 in cash (the asking price), and leave $500 of it in the center console of his car while he negotiated the deal. We pulled up, had a look at the car, and took it for a test drive. Before we got out of the car, my Dad told me to be quiet while he spoke to the owner. I'll never forget how my Dad talked to him. He kept his cool. He never got overly excited. He made a cash offer to the seller, and the seller countered. That old seller knew how bad this man's kid wanted this car. It was written all over my face, and the seller knew it. My Dad paid full price for the car. Even though $500 of the $1,500 was in the center console, the seller got his asking price from my father. Was it because my Dad was a sucker? Not a chance. My Dad knows this business better than anyone I know. Looking back, I realized that the seller knew how bad this man's kid wanted that car. It opened my eyes to the world of sales. And 25 years later, I can sell a starving dog off a meat truck.

I learned something about myself that day through my father's negotiation. I knew that if I could recognize at 16 years old how people instantly get attached to things, attach a monetary value to it through excitement, and then make an impulsive decision to buy it, that I could sell anything. My Dad could have got that guy to sell him that car for $1,000 easily. Especially if his boy wasn't standing there. He knows that and I know that. But he bought it for me anyway. I was his boy, and he knew that car was going to make me happy. He was my hero that day, and he knew it.

I also wrote this manual for you, the aspiring private party car salesman. I've learned success in this industry, and I want to pass my knowledge and experience to you. Buying and selling cars is not work to me. It is play.

It is my hope that you can take the tools and advice that I've provided you in this manual; while applying it in a way that makes you profitable, hard-working and honest. I also hope you have a shit load of fun while you do it. Here's to you and your journey. Best of luck and God bless.

Printed in Great Britain
by Amazon